STAR

WAKA

also by Robert Sullivan

Jazz Waiata (AUP, 1990)
Pike Ake! (AUP, 1993)
Maui: legends of the outcast (illustrated by Chris Slane, Godwit, 1996)
Manoa: homelands (editor, with Reina Whaitiri, Hawai'i, 1997)

STAR WAKA

Robert Sullivan

AUCKLAND UNIVERSITY PRESS

Some of the poems in this book have appeared in the following publications:
Growing up Maori (Tandem Press, 1998), *JAAM, Landfall, Nga Tai Puhoro,
Quadrant, Rampike, Riding the Meridian* (www.heelstone.com/meridian),
Trout (www.auckland.ac.nz/lbr/trout/trout.htm), *Wasafiri* (London),
Windsor Literary Review (Ontario).

The author is grateful to the English Department at the University of Auckland, and Creative
New Zealand, for a literary fellowship in 1998 which enabled him to complete this book.

First published 1999
Reprinted 2000, 2003, 2011, 2012, 2013

Auckland University Press
University of Auckland
Private Bag 92019
Auckland 1142
New Zealand
www.press.auckland.ac.nz

© Robert Sullivan

ISBN 978 1 86940 213 6

Publication is assisted by ARTS COUNCIL OF NEW ZEALAND *TOI AOTEAROA*

Front cover illustration: 'Boats of the Friendly Isles', in George W. Anderson,
*A New, Authentic, and Complete Collection of Captain Cook's First, Second, Third and Last Voyages,
1768–1780*, London, 1784.

Cover design by Christine Hansen
Printed by Printlink Ltd, Wellington

CONTENTS

NOTE

large *and* I wrote *Star Waka* with some threads to it: that each poem must have a star, a (waka) or the ocean. This sequence is like a waka, members of the crew change, the rhythm and the view changes – it is subject to the laws of nature.

There are three sections, indicated by the change in title numbering from Roman to Arabic to 'waka' numbering. Occasionally a poem's numbering breaks into another part of the sequence.

There is a core of one hundred poems, and 2001 lines.

For references to Maori mythology see Margaret Orbell's *Encyclopedia of Maori Mythology*. Other references are built into the text.

He karakia timatanga

A prayer to guide waka out the throat,
between Hawaiiki's teeth, the last green speckled

glove of coast, past upthrust knee and rock toe
in the distance to paddle and sail toward sunset –

when each crack in the house of the sun
is submerged – doors and windows cloaked by night,

charred sky where stars become arrows,
lit signs travelling across a black zone.

A prayer to hold lashings and fittings close
amid the swelled guts of Tangaroa.

A prayer to scoop out sustenance –
sweet fish caught by divers in bright saltwater

marinaded in coconut and hunger. A prayer
to keep food for the two week trip to Aotearoa,

gourds intact, yam and taro and kumara gods alert
to the slap and grab of a restless swell –

whether in the breast or seabed. A prayer, a declaration,
for quick land, straight seas, and health

of all parts celestial, temporal and divine:
food music and drink of this star waka –

the chanted rhythms
hoea hoea ra

storms
hoea hoea ra

1

a thousand years
hoea hoea ra

fleet mothers of tales
hoea hoea ra

I greet you in prayer oh star oh waka . . .
and pray for your combination here.

He karakia mo korua, e te waka, e te whetu o te ao nei.
Star and waka, a prayer for you both.

a prayer
to you
both, this
waka, this
star

star

2

i

Men rest their oars at night –   [*large oral*]
sailing into (paua) plump fowl, sweet
water, miracles of earth, land rolling
from hills into skies, land large enough
for lakes, enough to gather people in,
a feast for a forest of gods hitting sky.

Star waka is a knife through time. Crews
change, language of each crew changes,
as fast as sun burns ground, and tongues curse him.
Crews take longer, yet learn less about makers
of waka, meanings of star. Inheritors
of body, watched by spirits watching star.

Star hangs on ears of night, defining light.   [*expresses emotion - ; or :*]
Hear sounds of waka knifing time – (aue) again,
what belongs to water belongs to blood. Crews leap aboard
leap out, with songs of relations and care
to send them. Whole families have journeyed here,
they continue the line. The bottom line

is to know where to go – star points.
(Kaituki) counts stroke. (Tohunga)   [*Priest/clergyman*]   [*person who keeps time*]
who dwells beyond law, finds star.
System is always there for waka.
Star rises and falls with night.
So guidance system attached.

Belief system of heart. And tide.
In ancient days navigators sent waka between.
Now, our speakers send us on waka. Their memories,
memory of people in us, invite, spirit,
compel us aboard, to home government, to centre:
(Savai'i) (Avaiki) Havaiki, Hawaiiki, from where we peopled

[*'island in samoa*]   [*name of homeland (spiritual, ancestral)*]

3

Kiwa's Great Sea. We left home by a thousand
different stars, but just one waka takes us back.
Let us regroup. We have never travelled further –
just one star stays familiar in the heavens now.
Tamanui sun dribbles from sky. How will we ever settle
this cold place? Makariri Will our high magic work here?

'loss of cultural ppl

And when waka reaches Aotearoa again,
empty, we know it has come for more –

and when waka reaches Europe
we know it has lost some more –

and when craft work on waka
descends into varnish and paint it has lost some more –

more times the waka leaves full
we lose more –

and more

iii About some of the crew

He takes notes about his history and culture, even his own family
he takes notes about. He tries to hit the right ones
every time he speaks about them – he does his best
to compliment and complement their abilities,
the way they looked and what they looked at.
Sometimes a few cracks appear in the waka:
someone was a murderer, or someone was not all
that they seemed. To the interested, cracks appear on
the same scale, are worthy of same judgement.
To hide these judgements in little letters is their fate.

iv 2140AD *solar eclipse*

Waka reaches for stars – mission control clears us for launch
and we are off to check the guidance system
personally. Some gods are Greek to us Polynesians,
who have lost touch with the Aryan mythology, — *god of sky/heaven*
but we recognise ours and others – Ranginui and his cloak,
and those of us who have seen *Fantasia* know Diana
and the host of beautiful satyrs and fauns. — *hide sun*

lost touch w/ white myths

We are off to consult with the top boss,
to ask for sovereignty and how to get this
from policy into action back home.
Just then the rocket runs out of fuel –
we didn't have enough cash for a full tank –
so we drift into an orbit we cannot escape from
until a police escort vessel tows us back

and fines us the equivalent of the fiscal envelope
signed a hundred and fifty years ago.

They confiscate the rocket ship, the only thing
all the iwi agreed to purchase with the last down payment.

v Honda Waka

Today I surrendered the life
of my Honda City
to a wrecker in Penrose for $30.

I bought it seven years ago for $6000.
It has rust in the lower sills,
rust around the side windows –
on the WOF inspection sheet it says:
'this car has bad and a lot of rust . . .'

That car took me to Uncle Pat's tangi in Bluff.
We stopped and gazed at Moeraki, — towns
the dream sky, on the way.   island NZ

A friend followed us in it on the way
to National Women's for Temuera's birth
(we were in her huge Citroen).

We went to Otaki, and Wellington,
in the Honda to visit family.

The Honda took me to Library School
perched next to Victoria Uni.

I drove Grandad across the creek in the Honda
at night after the family reunion bash.

Temuera's first car seat was in the Honda.
That Honda has seen a high percentage

of my poetry.
Now I have left it behind.

Shooting pains, or are they growing,
how does one enumerate and describe
a feeling? – should one resort to the military
analogy as outlined in Colonel Bridge's — battle, 1905
journal (there he goes again, referring
to the massacre as if he doesn't talk about it
enough – let the event lie boy, don't bore
the reader with the petty tale – it's all
in the Turnbull Library anyway, I'm sure
they'd want to read it when they're in
the mood) OR SHOULD ONE TELL
THE TRUTH IN CAPITAL LETTERS
(cut it *sic*) or should one concentrate
on the beauty of the waka slicing
through concentration, through the vision
of the mind, lighting the architecture
of every dwelling, beauty of physical story,
water worn lines of brown bodies
sliding close to one another,
dipping and rising toward shore?

vii Reconnaissance

Highlights of the forest of the Lord Tane [god of forests & birds]
were logged for the fleet. Fleet transport
and weaponry, food baskets and ancestors,
technology and carving: a greatness of hulls

and sails – ships for the mission – settlers going
to ground thousands of miles south-west, taking
their divinities, agriculture, animals, to inhabit
the strangeness of climate and soil reported

by the first expedition. The waka represent ancestors
in name and form. Their names are invoked today
and bind Maori people. Waka fight for yesterday
like it is tomorrow; war cries of orators line marae [alliteration]

with subjective recollections. Speakers
point out borders of land, which waka went
where, who guard harbours – voices modelling
land into history and lineage, driving up

highways of legend – much art is visual:
displays of beauty accessible to all
but the symbolism remains Maori
and will always be for Maori.

repetition
diction

I cannot make this like maker of waka –
reach into my heart
heal wood of its rough cuts

take what isn't mine to *take*

whittling and whittling

No

lines decked with paua

No

wooden crowns turned to warriors' bowels

dreaming of the beauty of the vessel

alliteration

fleets filling lakes and harbours

riding rivers in judgement

waka everywhere –

taking their contents to the settlements

what did they carry?
how can I tell you in confidence?

why is it that each time I stand
I sway? and the crew sways too?

star waka is in every waka –
land fell a thousand years ago

yet waka still searches for star
among all people
who have become stars

made stars in patterns on wood
and the justice of heaven

(which is black

remember

repetition

and he tries to remember
but remembering is for things
of experience

these things he hasn't experienced:

the timing of a hundred

following birds across an Ocean

diving into the Ocean
and coming back up

how huge an Ocean is

composing chants

to move people

across the Ocean

to set out from Hawaiiki

knowing the return is death

x Goldie (1)

he pads around downtown

spots the Toi Tamaki
Heritage Gallery's picture

of the starving lost waka crew –
so realistic, 'on the spot' –

proof of early
anthropological puddings

just look at it,
where are the women,
the crops, tools, material
for settlement?

hey they were paddling
round the ocean

when they bumped
into Aotearoa
and were canvassed –

must be their account

repetition
alliteration

he and I suggest ways of narrating a story of waves

a billion billion of them to borrow a phrase
borrowed from the infinite numbers available

in telling an infinite story lapping the shapes
formed round land – a set of keys on a lap

landing there by mistake – a slip
and it all piles into the ocean mistook

for a reclamation declaimed by the tumbling
mumbling tongues of salinity

at a beach which heads for a context
a breach into the canon of beaches

writing in sand obscured by puffs
and gulls and tide's own cursive

curling lickity ups and lollipop downs
through the otherwise metronomic

glassiness then swelling then rough
to high waves and back down

to the ground or to the rocks again
and again the saline solution

 We hear a lot in Auckland these days
about the cost of the viaduct basin

the benefits accrued from the Cup challenge
various economic analyses: tourists

property exposure capital: the Americans
are really doing their homework

before they decide to colonise us
(but this time I really mean most kiwis

i.e. 85.1% of the population according
to the 1996 census) it doesn't mean

much to the rest it's still going to be
a colony

xiii Rough Cuts

the strokes slow, start cutting the drink

becalmed by tired arms

billowing at a tangent

we need a flying fox to new land

hook our mast and glide

like our descendants in skies

who have histories

backwards and forwards

our descendants who will secure

discoveries and communicate

to their descendants the value

of wonders they will find

allowing us – the ancestors –

to navigate *our* history

down lines

xiv Ka huri ahau ki te reo o te ao pouri

And morning yields to the purpose of the day.

Bright blood, the sun a clot tying darkness.

Waka of death duels death's waka.

The event chokes blood lines –

to civilized time and *lex romanum*.

The threats, curses, fingers pointing
at me, descendant of the crew
of one death waka,

pinch every nerve,
make me sad and proud

that I am an ambassador,
representative of all they surveyed.

And confused, very confused.

Why did these things happen?

Why are these things put
on me?

Where does it end?
At least

I am learning my history,
the people

who lie within me.

Let anyone challenge
our place again.

xv Sullivan Whanau

The grass at Te Kaaretu was renowned
for its softness – our ancestors would line
their whare with it for bedding. Today we are
gathered up like clumps of Kaaretu grass,
made soft by the gathering, and we line
the whare nui at Pihareinga, Te Kaaretu,
with our bedding once again.

I learn Arapeta's song, *e tuwhera atu nei,*
te awa o Taumarere . . . our ancestral river
of Taumarere opens here, although of course
we had settlements at Matauwhi and Kororareka –
the first New Zealand capital – we were
one of the first tribes to be affected
by westernisation. Today we are following

the river, tracing the paths of our people,
the great names and the previously unknown,
trying to find the first Sullivan who gave us
his name early last century. What was his
first name? who did he marry? why did he stay here?
was he marooned? was it a woman?
what was his waka? These questions remain to date.

But there are tears at this reunion.
The speeches are from everyone here,
we introduce ourselves as the special branches
of the whanau. We move around
like the four winds, but when we gather
at Te Kaaretu, we are anchored
and hold fast to one another.

19

Waka 16 Kua wheturangitia koe

appear upon horizon / you / (you(?) / you star above the horizon / the horizon / repetition

Beloved
sent to Hawaiiki
to become a star
who guides
dreamers to reality

to become a star
portrait on the cloak
of a night on whose
shoulders rest
dreams

of a restless people
who dream white
waves of currency
waka rides
and falls

black and blue
with only stars
to point away since
sun and moon
are tagged for domination

yet stars are
ancestors
they are stars
our ancestors
and we will be stars

like kauri
totara
kahikatea
rimu
awa

trees / used to / tattoo / white pine / large forest / tree / moss / river

tapped for fire
sapped for gum
used for battle
construction materials
veins into dams

where the power
of the land powers
a mechanical culture
strange ships in the sky
air filled with radiation

we are vacuumed into this
culture of menace to the land
we are told we would do this too if
we had the technology
and our people do it

to the land for people
by people and this land
joins the congress of scars
on the planet a culture
of urban decay and renewal

a culture of dead capitals
sucking the life out of new
cities a culture that knows
no boundaries has only
prophecies called strategies

and stars look down on this and eyes
of divinities
look down on stars
and eyes
of the powerless look up

but only at night
when machines
lighten blackness
when many stars
are lost in the lightning

except in the papakainga
from tops of pa
from middle of ocean
from these places stars
meant to be seen can be

village / communal Maori land

20

standard of usage words

in English the waka
is a canoe
but the ancestral waka
were as large
as the European barks
of the eighteenth century explorers

size isn't the key factor here
it is the quality of the crews
their similar systems of navigation
the common purpose of settlement

and the labelling which is in English
which I do not need to spell out
except to say that it is still very
difficult to procure word processors

that have a set of macronised vowels
and subeditors who do not pluralise
Maori loan words although most have
ceased italicising them
to give a sense of inclusion
in one context

in the other context
it is for purposes
of pacification

sticking a pipe
through Stonehenge –
that's what it is
to direct that Mangere's *[handwritten: mountain (shores of Manukau Harbor)]*
ancient stone fields
have a sewerage pipe
cut through them

it is a violation of the lifeblood
of its guardians
to pour excrement
through one of the few
sacred areas left

in the region must be wrong
it is wrong isn't it?
don't you think it is wrong?
who thinks it is right?
is this extraordinary?

we are told *ordinariness*
is the standard in justice –
yet the word *Maori*
means *ordinary*

this
is a rearguard action –
up shit creek without a paddle
– who'd want to put a waka in that!

xix

man from
myth

Rata felled the tree
without leave from Tane

god of forests
+ birds

and so the leaves, chips
twigs etcetera

were reassembled each
evening – the hollow

waka shell undone
until thanks were given –

in the modern day
we have a PM

who asks Maori to give
thanks
for the settlement

process – the process
undoes the waka alright

but it puts back empty
trunks all over the land –

some of them
still standing

xx a whakapapa construction

not the ski-field I'm afraid

or talk of Rata descended from Tawhaki

descended from Maui Tikitiki a Taranga

or even mention of the nights –

the great night the long night –

not the intensity of blacknesses involved

in coming through the layers –

not the lines dangling from the heavens

Tawhaki at one end his beloved above him –

these lines are a whakapapa –

in themselves – ten years

of door knocking and practice

on roughs and finishes –

pushed to fluidity – one knows

the narrator should be quite dead

yet in a whakapapa the last line

should be the speaker's

kia ora

[handwritten annotations:]
semi-supernatural — associated lightning thunder
Polynesian characters of narratives
descent/reciting descent
hello

xxi Te ao marama *[handwritten: the bright moon]*

Aotea *[handwritten: Great Barrier Island]*

Square
        where the riot started
the closest I got was picking up Dad
from work in Newmarket –
the police cordon began
a hundred metres
up Khyber Pass
                then watching it all
on telly.

In the Centre I saw *Don Giovanni*
starring Kiri Te Kanawa,
and a few other operas.

In the old Town Hall I asked
a question about seniority
at the NLGOU stopwork meeting.

Often I cross the Square
on my way home – skateboarders
try to scare pedestrians,
but I ignore them. Today
I noticed the banners
for a Maori convention,
                big business.

It reminds me of seventh form Classical Studies,
the spectacle of the Colosseum pit
filled with water for mock
                naval battles;
and *panem et circenses*.

Kurahaupo
Kura kaupapa, kohanga reo, kura tuarua –
all schools to advance the Maori culture.

[handwritten annotations: crew on canoe from Hawaiki, said to be ancestor; school; policy; nursery; voice; high school]

Kurahaupo was a waka. Recently
waka have performed a similar function.

They have travelled with us
through the evolution of legends

and the tongues our legends use.
Waka spring from our unconscious,

the deep structure of Polynesia
to reappear in the modern world.

In 1990 I went to *the* Waitangi celebrations.
Walking through Paihia to the Treaty Grounds

I passed waka taua, pahi, waka ama;
fibreglass, wooden, carved and painted –

[handwritten annotations: war canoe; ooze; outrigger canoe]

these waka were paddled, shipped,
trucked from all over on an oily rag.

Their resurrection propels our iwi
into the new age: vehicles for a revival.

xxiii Formats (1)

sepia
paint
text
video
dat
email
html
doc files
water
cd rom
cd photo
    waka

ego in the strokes

restorations
revivals
hands-on chisels
hands to paddles
    each motion
creating motion
across Raukawa — *tribe*
down Te Wai Pounamu — *Island*
waka for the foothold
to haul a fish

ee ya ha ha!

the hauling

xxv power/powerlessness

waka cuts it
  Maori in magazines
remarkable
  sensational
sports stars

Maori models wear groovy fashion
single studded ears
indigenous beauty

at the second Maori expo

dark green lipstick

sips from silver

coffee cups

xxvi

I rest *Star Waka* on Nga Waka *Maori*
by Anne Nelson, white tipped

paddles raised to catch
the setting sun
which sets them
yellow, red bodies

the colour
of the waka,
men hongi'ing the nose
of the waka,

faces touching before
their launch
into the mind

of Tangaroa.

[handwritten annotations: "breathe", "ancestor of sea + fish"]

and the mind of Tangaroa
is disturbed by his brother

Tawhirimatea – turns
his back on greenstone seas

god of
weather

into alcoholic vortices
focuses

on whirlpool Tangaroa
what a spewer!

until brother tires
of being a blowhard

retreats to distance
where offspring of the real

perpetrator – Tane Mahuta –
with genetic memory

ancestor
of forests &
birds

of fights and their patterns
find paua seek hapuka

glide along greenstone
lines of thought

xxviii Hooked

some say the South Island

is a waka

the North Island is a fish

and the Cook Strait cable (I reckon)

is the only link between them

Waka 29 (*waka taua*) — war canoe

water spirit / guardian

A taniwha brushes the sides

waka pitches

uenuku touches the eyes

rainbow / ancestor associated w rainbow/important ancestor

rainbow / ancestor

33

xxx

in three weeks I turn 30

in three decades
men have landed
on the moon

women have become prime ministers

thousands gained PhDs

trillions of dollars circulated

soft wood forests grown to maturity

52 x 30 no.1 hit singles

mortgages completely repaid

the microcomputer has developed

and I have achieved feelings
I didn't have before –
what about you?

xxxi

spirals in the (tauihu) — bow/figurehead
(of canoe)

signatures in water

waka cutting each other's wake

signing
xxxxxxxxxxxxxxxxxxxxxxxxx

visible from the air

someone in a helicopter

took a photo

counted the signatures

later

xxxii herenga waka

we all belong to a waka

those of us lucky enough to trace

our whakapapa back to Hawaiiki

into times of divinity when all things

Maori were also divine

but we belong to an ugly side too

collected slaves and wars

we were imperfect gods

not unlike the antiquarian

beasts and gladiators of Europe

but the waka carries us all

above the water

a poem about the weight of wood

native trees in their entirety

not like trees in H. R. Puffenstuff

(the talking variety)

but the energy within them

pushing out leaves in Spring, sap etc.

(like your email says)

energy derived from the heater up there

and the pull of the moon (not proven

but surely?) this heat goes into waves

and the things above them – air itself –

which gyres invisibly except for the things

it touches – leaves, branches, buildings

foundations for natural and human

constructions

some set to float by the measure

of the circumference of seas –

displaced in degrees

by wood and by land

Our cat's name was Goldie,
daughter of Black Jet,
sister of Black Jet Junior and Gingy –
their brother
       was Spotty.

C. F. Goldie was and remains
a famous New Zealand
painter. He still takes the rap
      for *The Arrival of the Maoris* –
in the current exhibition at the Heritage Gallery
that piece is placed with his French paintings,
partly so that it is separated
from the Maori portraits.

The ancestors in the portraits
look grim, with few exceptions.
The ones in *Arrival*
look destitute. I cannot speak

as a direct descendant
of a Goldie subject,
as my ancestors were depicted
by Lindauer.

to discover an island must be amazing
new resources – water, timber, land –
the claim of discovery when you return home
you'd really put on your glad rags
so this thing about the unhappy crews
who shipwreck by chance
doesn't make sense does it?
how did they procreate if it wasn't deliberate?
it's a gender issue I realise

the introduction of large
European ships to New Zealand waters
made quite an impact
ballistical even
yet we must think
about the hardy voyagers
life in Europe was no pleasure cruise
they must have had desperate
existences back home
I acknowledge their bravery
to sail over the edge of the world
into Hades
the infernal Greek and Latin-ness
of many headed creatures
sirens to put them on the lips
of story-tellers
they must have never considered
for a second that they would return

your majesty
arikinui — captain of canoe
taumata — surname/hill(?)
etcetera

we have sighted them

who?

we have seen *them*
again
     and
       again
running around
on their waka

different people

who *runs* on a waka?
have you lost your heads?
gone porangi? crazy

esteemed one
here they come

38 fleurs de lis

do not be afraid –
I have seen them too
Tangaroa has delivered a dish

a top-heavy banquet
plying our waves
a European maitre'd

ourselves boys/ girls

our omniscient descendants
will liken them to gingerbread

which we will snap while they
sit on our backs

ooh la la

39 *A wave*

On the NativeNet email discussion list
someone listed the atrocities

committed after Columbus.
five hundred years later

and the Papal Bull that begat them
on vellum still stands.

Men women and children
were spiked in His name.

This nauseating wave
splashes today –

nations only traceable
by their DNA –

justice in mixed
blood.

40

I imagine my friend walking on reservation land

near the Great Lakes

of South-West Ontario

ice in Winter driving the roar

of Spring

and the Summer's day

before the sun

reaches Autumn and thoughts

of eternal Summer inside

are learnt lines

enthusiasm for words again

in her presence

and in her absence

lines singing of a free life

there

41

cutting across Grey Lynn Park
with the open scars of collapsed storm drains

warning signs great sheets of iron
across the struggling earth

I find fields on the far side
it is moving

I am moved by the space
in the city

(our backyard is so small)

am forced to think of nature
the changing course (Sonnet xviii)

I think above all of Canada
and oceanic fields

42

Into the new age the waka glides
through halls of mirrors

past the birthplace Rangiatea
across waves of blood – Mau,

takata Maoli, sovereignty
buried in the franchise contracts – oh

we are peoples united by more
than genes, by more than the tongues

of our ancestors reciting names
of great ones, we are united

by culture, by the psyche
of our cultures, our closeness

even in this age turned
against the sacred

43

The South Pacific Forum met recently in Rarotonga.

CHOGM meets soon – they've readmitted Fiji.

The powerful and the powerless

across (internationally) and vertically (internally).

Power is on show in Polynesia regularly.

the Polynesian branch of the Austronesian
languages has a common parent
        Proto-Polynesian

which features a decimal number system

and a large list of words still found

throughout Polynesia

Captain Cook had Tupaia, a Tahitian interpreter
aboard who communicated with the tangata
whenua

Saint Kateri says Hawaiians understand Maori

just think of the geography

we reached South America
because kumara, our staple root crop, is from there

perhaps Hawaiians commuted to America – what

given the Polynesian track record –
could have stopped them?

how did we do it? don't we indicate the depth
of our guardianship by travelling

to *Japan* to retrieve original kumara stocks
from scientists just recently, this decade,

to ensure our intellectual
property (the root strain)

and diversity (biological)
are maintained?

the ingredients of the story –
a fantasy palace like the Civic
filled with dreams
and a winking ceiling
a dome to navigate the heavens by
imagine in 1929 414 elephants monkeys
salamanders proscenium arches
lions minarets according
to Jonathan Dennis's guest
(it is true I have seen it)
dancers clothed only in gilt paint
people were conceived in the Civic
what drove the architects to this
ornamented grandeur?
The greatest theatre in the dominion . . .
A national institution . . .
Its brothers and sisters called the Regent,
St James, the Embassy, or simply
dead. The Auckland City Council will restore it,
but 'mask' the proscenium arch, the winged globe,
the winking lions. What kind of vandals are they?
They will restore it as a theatre for musicals –
but it's a cinema! A waka is a vehicle for navigators,
a pitched symbol of the genius of our people,
its physical representatives held in glory.
Auckland doesn't deserve the Civic.

it is feasible that we will enter

space
colonise planets call our spacecraft *waka*

generous

perhaps name them after the first fleet
erect marae transport carvers renew stories
with celestial import

establish new forms of verse
free ourselves of the need for politics
and concentrate on beauty

like the release from gravity
orbit an image until it is absorbed
through the layers of skin

spin it
sniff and stroke the object
become poetic

oh to be in that generation
to write in freefall picking up the tools
our culture has given us

and to let them go again
knowing they won't hit anyone
just stay up there

no longer subject to peculiarities
of climate the political economies
of powers and powerless

a space waka
rocketing to another orb
singing waiata to the spheres

47

beams emanate from Mother Mary's
head – the baby in its crib

donkey expectantly leans his head
this frame is in our bedroom

yet there are emanations
from the breathing of our daughter Eileen

dim light exiting from Temuera's room
they frame our thoughts

at times lifting our eyelids
when they are shut for business

Anne, lying next to me, feeds her again
she turns around and sleeps

kia pai to moemoea Eileen Te Aho
little star

48 (Bright 1)

Temuera says the sun
looks like a piece
of kauri gum

*tree
used to
tattoo*

49 (environment 1)   *spelling*

will the next makers of waka
live in submarines
[so threatened by the mechanical heat
of organised industry

treated like residents
of the Clyde Dam's precincts
gold mines turned to sepia
populations moved to hills by sermons?

from the top
Clinton to reduce the gas by 2011
back to the ozone hole of 1990
(wish I could turn the clock back

wait   tell the younger me
(taihoa) but write more
about home
before he's dammed.

into poems clutching reeds
waka bobbing above)

53

It is the star to every wand'ring bark,
Whose worth's unknown, although his height be
taken.

A compass pointing North past Canada
to push this crew furthest South with angles,
crow's nest for a shout, the headland!
A mass the rest of the crew discover –
people to convert, flat stretches, rolls of fat
turned up to summits, dense green
of black intensity, the only common law
Newtonian – a karaka berry will fall from its tree.

Aged heads of kauri are the afros of the land,
huge rastas, proudest beings of these South Seas.
Converted to spars for the crown fleets
victories for Downing St. A new reggae nation
ready for tilling and sharing; imagine, oh beasts,
birds of Europe, oh vegetables, fields,
the great yields for roots and guts we have discovered!

Begin the definition of these islands –
let circumnavigation precede acquisition.
Let ambiguities of Tahitian allow us excuses
for our reasons – musketry and the barrel
to raise the sheilas' piupiu the parson
to peel men off for their eyes.

What is gallantry these days
but by Mitsubishi? Who interprets history?
Who stores the manuscripts and books
of the lost? In time's fair mind
we have objectivity, but for generations
it is no release from captivity – we are pharoah's
possessions, and as each pharoah succumbs

54

to the coin, dragging the bags
across the Tasman into the holy see,

we watch and wait for justice. Justice
for inclusion in the proletariat. Justice
for compliance by salary. Justice
for revoking our guardianship of all
the eye can see in the imposition
of adversarial law. Justice for our apathy.
Justice the person who sits at the bench.

We wait for the Justice Bus.
We wait for the Liberty Bus.
We watch the New Zealand First Bus
wheels go round and round
and the faces inside smiling
and waving round and round.
We're at the right Bus Stop.

The timetable says they should pull up.
But signal and you lose an arm.
Or it's the tourist bus. Or you're told
by your mates about the last time
they signalled and how it freaked them out.
Sometimes it's just plain tough to stand
on the street – everybody else has wheels.

Why turn and face the sun, knowing
that justice is going to run you down?
In the cool nights when stars slide
above street lamps, it's easy to look up –
much easier to think of waka crews
and hear in traffic the inside of a shell.

rainbow/
ancestor/goddess
associated w/
rainbow

(Uenuku) Bird Flight

Waka Light Dark Shift

Leaf Ocean Ocean Mist

my cousin Billy said to me on Friday
that he was going to navigate his way
up to Karetu (what a coincidence I thought
I must stick that in a poem)

community in Northland region of N island

we're going to spend Christmas there
this year (1997) for perhaps the last time
disturbing (like the state of the health system)

it will be Eileen's first visit
Temuera's second
Anne's third

It will be somewhere in the thirties or forties
for me – most of the visits in my childhood

but my mother is from Karetu
and that is how I know the place
through all the stories she's told me

like Grandpa Turi bringing a slab of icecream
back for the kids after the races on Saturday
about Nanny Pu who lived to be over a hundred
and only spoke Maori
about her mother's hard life
or living in the country without a pair of shoes
milking the cows by hand before going to school
about the men and women of Karetu
and some of their terrible secrets
even I won't tell
that's why I go back because of my mother
who planted Karetu in me

not just because of my ancestors
buried in the cemetery and the cave nearby
whose waka navigated to the soil there

53

island island

no-man

island island

whale

island island

Robert

carved shaped loved floating totara

coral, sea, tree

in danger? - environmental concerns that come up in other places in book

54 waka *rorohiko* — computer

voice/lang/ speech

I heard it at Awataha Marae
in te reo – waka rorohiko – computer
'computer waka', about a database
containing whakapapa. Some tapu genealogy/lineage
information, not for publication. saved info.
A dilemma for the library culture
of access for all, no matter who, how,
why. A big Western principle stressing
egalitarianism. My respects.
However, Maori knowledge brings many
together to share their passed down wisdom
in person to verify their inheritance;
without this unity our collective knowledge
dissipates into cults of personality.

55 *Araiteuru*

The crew of this waka, touched by daylight,
turned to stone up and down the east coast

of the South Island – some became mountains,
Mt Torlesse, Mt Somers, Mt Tasman, Mt Cook –

forests, ranges, pillars and hills. Of course
I am translating names here. A hill in this part

of the country, for example, would probably
be taller than Auckland's Mt Eden, which

is roughly as tall as the Sky Tower
which consumed vast amounts of gravel

in its construction. Perhaps some of this
was extracted from the Araiteuru's crew?

Kai Tahu, to whom my father belongs,
restored one mountain 'Aoraki' (Mt Cook).

Canoe from Hawaiki, dieded's to Matakaea

repetition

Waka 56 A Double-Hulled Waka

i

Which begins as they do telling stories –
    from heavenly Moeraki where, parked,
I gazed at a big wall of sea and sky,
    earth a ledge beneath a bright veil crossing
Paradise. A Western Paradise true
    to its own logic, boulders parked like stops
across the text. My head filled with heaven,
    I drove and drove, wheel in my hands bouncing.
The image bounced round inside me for years
    like a prayer-wheel powered by water
coming out of the ground through me – spring
    filled with eels nibbling my insides. Maui's
tuna of the meiosis, wrestling his
    descent, his own meiosis, the people.

And the next story beginning a line
    dangling from glow worms on lime formations,
points of light fishing for winged insects
    on hope – for moon, sun, stars – not devouring
worms. They live in darkness, manufacture
    their own light. They possess beauty their fans
die like lovers for. I know these lovers,
    felt the breeze raise a veil from a sunset
internalised. Lime spears caverns. Worm mouths.
    Each bit a wriggle along existence.
Grandiose. A stretch across plates for salt.
    Dissembled in the gut, shared out to senses,
tissue, organic stuff, all contribute
    to each chemical and animal light.

Scales of light vary, measuring speed, lux,
     changes: physicists think we are stardust.
Down to a person. Massive and modest
     stars recycled in the cosmos – we are
reassembled versions of long dead stars.
     Now science imitates art. Once artists
were scientists too. Today vice versa.
     Da Vinci, for example, observed candles,
designed helicopters. Today, the Beeb
     ran a story about a scientist
exhibiting pictures of molecules:
     a silk molecule next to a silk dress;
chlorophyll next to a plant. Everything
     a collection of tiny connections.

For beauty has delightful components.
The molecule of water sliding by
molecules of waka, powered by breeze
molecules in muscles, on sails – its scales
notes on the firmament, melodious
oration, song, rhythm of pahu, flute,
feet braced on boards swinging torso, elbow,
thought. This thought passed down lengths of men
                              through earth –
we came by waka, we leave by waka,
pass it on. The influences of wind
on waves can be immense, high walls scraping
valleys in the heart, constricting throats. Crews
scraped themselves, bled prayers, so holiness
remained – a caravan on dry seabed.

ii

[handwritten: feathers of huia huia (bird, now extinct)]

Contents of waka huia, treasure chests,
    are highly prized. *Waka huia* on tv,
a Maori language show, has just broadcast
    its 400th episode – preserving
eloquence, movement, airs, graces, *noblesse*
    of our leaders, finest men and women,
on video forever. In Maori.
    Only 14 episodes subtitled.
To understand one's culture one must speak
    the language of its poetry, world
philosophy, reach untranslated
    ambiguities. For language deals out
meaning. Meaning is the star above our
    species. Specifically, our waka

follows this. Meaning is food for chiefs.
    Succulent hearts steaming in hot ovens
of earth. The land fortified a thousand
    years with our blood. We grew tall here. We must
reclaim gifts of mouth, example. Faces
    must drink in faces, lap up, ripple, splash
each other. Make moko in the wrinkles,
    warriors for ourselves, for our people,
leaping from pits into bright daylight
    defying the culture of the death
of our culture. Spray out its narrative
    with whakairo. In many places *[handwritten: carving]*
we share ancestry, jokes, communities
    of spirit grown up over settlement –

and so this waka has passed its
thousandth line, Maori and Pakeha,
stars, knowledge of places only referred –

but only lines glide here on salt water,
come out in commanding the stroke – again,
stroke again, stroke, stroke, stroke again, again . . .

Waka 57 El Nino Waka

Among the compasses of navigators –
star compass, wind compass, solar compass –
a compass based on currents, such was
the reliability of the sea. Today the sea
is unreliable. Whatever the reason
for El Nino – deforestation of North and South America,
for example – El Nino has burst into the sea
as rapidly as it has burst into our popular culture
and our livelihoods: droughts and floods and storms
around the rim of the Pacific, the great fluid
of the compass a-bubble with this burst artery.
I can see its origins, as you can. Lack
of respect for the planet. The planet, as you are aware,
is not only our mother, but the mother of all
living creatures here, from the latest computer virus
to the greatest of the primates. She carries us
through the universe. These things
are simple, something that human beings
have known throughout their human beingness,
which we know is brief compared to our mother's being.

El Nino is blood from our mother. She bleeds
internally, then from ocean into air in a maelstrom.
Then we send people with cameras: to show lakes
turn to mud, to show a tower or a field of cane
snap in a hurricane. I don't have any answers
for El Nino. I am too small. These words
are too affected by El Nino to possess
any objectivity at all.

Waka 58 Waitangi Day

Our organic milk carton's expiry date
is 6 February 1998. A found poem
sent by one of the gods of the harvest,
slipped unsuspectingly into my Foodtown trolley
by Haumietiketike perhaps? just like bumping
into an artist in the Grey Lynn aisles late at night,
swapping notes about our 21-month-old daughters –
another found poem. To think at the time
I didn't see 6 February being scanned
at the checkout, getting stuck in a plastic bag,
being jostled along with the rest of the groceries.
And what about all the other dates, the possible
found poems on consumables – Easter on the honey,
2001 a space odyssey on the noodles,
Jim Morrison's birthday on the candles?
What a far reach 6 February has,
all the way to the waka navigators
and all the way back . . .

[handwritten annotation: offspring of Ranginui (sky God)]

I have begun reading *The Maori Canoe*.
The detail is gratifying. Discussions
of the double canoe, the single canoe
                     with outrigger,
the single canoe with no outrigger,
various descriptions and commentaries,
all gathered in one meeting place: *The Maori Canoe*.

To be fair to Best he did find the term *canoe*
an inadequate word, quoting from the copy of
Webster's available to him around 1925:
    A boat used by rude nations, formed of the trunk
    of a tree, excavated by cutting or burning into a
    suitable shape.
He found it, however, ' . . .scarcely advisable to employ
the native term of *waka . . .*' (p.18) without saying why.

I am still grateful to Best. He saw the beauty
in our stories. He noticed that names
of some constellations correspond with the names
of waka: Te Waka o Tama-rereti is Scorpio,
Te Waka o Mairerangi includes Antares.
He found it remarkable,
indeed these are in his introductory remarks,
that the stars were placed in Tama-rereti's waka
so that the sun and the moon
would not jostle them.

[handwritten margin notes: "Scorpius (constella-tion)" and "star (15th brightest)"]

66

He mentions ara moana too. The great path
resting on the sea's surface, a path set down
by the lips of the navigators who used every sense
about them to find the path that expands
and contracts between the compasses
of Polynesian culture, an accumulation halted
by literacy and modern navigation –
recorded as an afterthought by those Europeans
not overly preoccupied with other things,
and sifted out by people such as Best.

unwanted materials thrown overboard + washed ashore

wreckage of ship

The heights and shapes of waves, flotsam
and jetsam, indicate the direction of currents.

Lewis says that a line of jetsam clearly delineates
the meeting point of two currents –

so for instance, where the refuse from Taco Pronto
and the refuse from Burger King meet

should indicate the meeting point of currents halfway
around the globe (although I hear that Taco Pronto

is down to just one franchise in Auckland).
The McDonalds jetsam indicates nothing, of course.

Waka 61 Fragment
(adapted from Hetaraka Tautahi)

This is the paddle Te Roku-o-whiti
who stays close to the side
encircles the side
stands forward
flies ahead
springs onward
slaps Tangaroa's back
(who sometimes slaps back)

ancestor of sea, lakes, rivers + creatures (esp fish)

Waka 62 *A narrator's note*

There is no Odysseus to lead this fleet –
not even Maui who sent waka to their petrification,

the waka Mahunui, for instance, placed exactly
in the centre of the South Island at Maui's command.

I have only waka floating beneath the stars,
at night and in the day, directed by swells,

whose crews are sustained not by seabirds
or fish, but by memory – some in conflict

with the written record. I have seen waka only at rest.
They are beings worthy of the company they keep –

tohunga, to furnish voyagers with karakia, taniwha for security,
the very stars in motion with them.

I cannot provide you with a leader of the fleet.
This fleet navigated centuries. The names

of captains were known to their colleagues
as ancestors. The Pacific was a far-flung society

– waka, cocooned in Aotearoa,
stopped returning to Hawaiiki, dropped their sails,

clambered overland into rivers, burrowed
into mountains, reefs, flew into words

sung at tangi, polished speeches,
seen by the paua eyes of gods and ancestors

whose real eyes, blinking in the light
of their lives millennia and centuries ago,

saw the vehicles themselves –
spacecraft, oxygen tanks, caravans led by elephants,

vehicles of concept, exploration, sails a vortex
ribbed by people shouting names down into the Great Sea.

Waka 63 Venus

Point this poem to Kopua.

Please memorise it.

Waka 64

i

It's no irony that Waitangi means
crying waters, water of tears –

they pour from a height
their source as mysterious as the Nile's

mixed blood
adrenalin salt on skin

often my people's
although the individual owners

are beyond a DNA trace
while the drops of Waitangi
are mixed with rain

ii

they row the Waitangi waka
on Waitangi Day (which keeps
the theme of this sequence –
a waka or a star or ocean
in each poem)

Waka 65

He kakano i ruia mai i Rangiatea

[handwritten annotations: color/texture, shake/skatter, in Hawaiki, this way/from/since]

When the waka congregate at the high temple
of Taputapuatea, in Rangiatea,

when our priests are gathered
and permissions granted to proceed,

we will piece together our intelligence
from the two thousand year mission –

compare the methods, materials,
languages of the enterprise.

A great living Library of people,
trillions of brain cells indexed

from the heart, cross-referenced
through usefulness to life, powered

by the stuff of life itself. Among
these cells lie references to waka,

to waka ritual, methods of navigation,
knowledge of stars currents wind –

the great gathering place of spirits,
Te Hono i Wairua represents

[handwritten annotation: gathering place of spirits]

this knowledge – for after death
we know where to find Hawaiiki –

the living send them here
without directions.

Waka 66 Hokule'a

Masts flute sails out to mouth shapes
like beaks of taniwha coming from the sea
the only hint of people the rigging

water spirit

sweeping like vines from the canopy
of Tane's domain – they draw on the ocean
like taniwha straws whose sails

are taniwha gills in the breeze
while the prow (you know, the taniwha nose)
points home like an instinct as magnetic

as the grip of the people
on this taniwha's back

Waka 67 from We the Navigators

Boobies, noddies, terns – these and other birds
indicate the presence of land, most particularly
in the early morning and the evening when

they return home. They fly straight
to their perches. Some birds come out at night
to explore the waka. Depending

on the species you can rely on them for up
to fifty miles out. It's well documented
in the Pacific that frigate birds were used

to find land, and even as messenger birds
across islands. They'd get a feed of fish
at the other perch. Before writing, the messages

came in the form of pearls. Birds save lives.
Gatty wrote survival books based on bird sightings
for airmen forced down at sea: his *Raft Book* for instance,

and *South Sea Lore*, which was a combination
of Polynesian and Arab methods. The Arabs were
seafarers too of course, and came down into the Indian

Ocean. Their waka were called *prau*.
Who knows how far they got?

Is it a myth – the idea of Polynesia,
a colonial construct partitioning the Pacific?

What does it matter when there are other myths
that have more influence on our lives?

At least 'Polynesians' can embrace
a continuity outlined in genealogies stretching

back to the gods. Nga Puhi, for instance,
have Matahourua in Kupe's time, which was re-adzed

in his grandson Nukutawhiti's time to become
Ngatokimatawhaorua. In that case Polynesia returned
to Aotearoa

[Handwritten annotations:]
tribal group (Northland)
early visitor to NZ → Hawaiki
Canoe → Kupe Hawaiki
Canoe, used in migration to settle NZ
village, rural, Northland & Whangarei District

Waka 69 Kupe

Who was he? Why did he come here
of all places? Was he actually the first person

[handwritten: daughter of Toto, Cheif of Hawaiki.]

to arrive? One account has him coveting Kuramarotini,
who was already married to Hoturapa – the voyage being one

long elopement. Another has him chasing the great
pet octopus of Muturangi aboard Matahourua

[handwritten: navigator]

because it kept stealing the bait off his hooks.
For a safe return journey he sacrificed his son

Tuputupu-whenua here in the Spring of the World of Light.
Imagine such a thing. I could never do it.

[handwritten: divine/ semi- divine person/ land on NZ]

In *Nga Waka o Nehera* by Jeff Evans there is mention
of people already present in Aotearoa who Kupe visited,

namely Taikehu and his people at Patea. Kupe named many
places in Aotearoa, which the following poems

[handwritten: chief / town/ N Island]

describe, based on references in the *Journal of the Polynesian
Society* and other sources listed in Evans.

Anne Nelson tells of Hui Te Rangiora who came
before Kupe and sailed so far south he saw icebergs.

[handwritten: 7th C. navigator from Rarotonga]

That's a claim lodged well before Richard Pearse's flight
over the Wright Brothers or the first kiwi pavlova.

Waka 70

*Among the places and landmarks associated with Kupe and the
Matahourua expedition are the following . . .* (Evans, p.97)

i Matakitaki

Kupe talks to his daughter:
I was looking for hapuka I had summoned from the deeps,
when my eyes ascended white mountains in the distance,
I stared and stared – from this pile of common rocks which
I will remember as the place of Matakitaki (in Palliser Bay)

I find myself deleting the roll of names relating to Kupe,
listed in Evans: they are translatable without me, the sail

of Matahourua that needed replacing, the ure or penis
of Kupe which Smith says he 'scratched' while he sunbathed,

the names of waka bailers and anchors, his dogs,
his footprints left in clay – relics pointed out

for a millennium by learned people. Who am I to retouch
these icons of Kupe? He hardly needs rediscovery.

There is a Kupe in all of us, who struggles for love,
and with the forces of the deeps. I look for him.

[handwritten annotations: "big fish" (left margin); "Cape Palliser – S most point of N island" (right margin)]

Waka 71

Burt Reynolds has made his screen come-back
in *Boogie Nights*, getting an Oscar nomination to boot.

Likewise, so has outrigger canoeing. Competitors
in the World Sprints come from 28 different countries

in Oceania. New Zealand won eight gold medals in Samoa
in 1994. The national association is called Nga Kaihoe o Aotearoa.

Anne's cousin Gael joined a waka crew – I must
ask her about it. After the enthusiasm for waka toa in the 1990

sesquicentenary celebrations things have died down.
I only saw one waka toa on tv at Waitangi this year,

compared with the great fleet eight years ago. But the waka
will come back on show – they're always here anyway,

in the shapes of the land: the prow of the South Island
for instance is the Marlborough Sounds (see the fine carved detail?)

Kupe recommended journeying
to Aotearoa in October. The starpath

of Kopua (Venus) in late October
tracks almost directly from Rangiatea

to Aotearoa. It's amazing to see it on a chart.
The star navigation chart for 31 October 1985 depicts

Kopua to the north of Northland, Marama the moon
tracking between Moorea and East Cape (near Gisborne),

and Matariki (Southern Cross) tracking
south of Tahiti and south of Southland (Nelson, p.19).

Hawaikinui used methods such as wind streamers
of aute leaves (paper mulberry) which when bleached

become flurescent. The way they move
indicates deviations from course,

and of course, they can be used at night.
When the celestial bodies are obscured

there are the streamers – bearing
back thousands of years.

Waka 73 Gone fishing

I took Temuera fishing out at Orakei
yesterday. We got him a fishing rod
for his birthday. We brought morning tea,
fortunately, so the time was well spent
munching sammies and drinking
our drinks. Occasionally we saw
fish swimming above and around
our hooks, but not a nibble.
Other guys on the pier had sprat lines
which, when they cast them, looked
like sparkling schools flying through the air.
They seemed to be catching a few.

Temuera and I also saw the waka crews.
A crew of women rowed beyond the yacht
moorings towards Rangitoto. A crew of men
stayed in the basin trailing a Coca Cola flag.
Glad to see the multinationals
are sponsoring them. I'm all for it.

A yacht pulled up and disturbed the fish
so we packed up. A film crew were shooting
a film or a commercial – perhaps we'll be in it?

Waka 74 Sea anchor

In storms the waka would lower
a sea anchor halfway to help control

the vessel. In a way this poem
is a sea anchor. We are waiting

for a storm to pass, one preventing
control of the narrative.

There were other types
of punga (anchors).

A light anchor was used
to determine a current.

And of course there were anchors
to hold a vessel in place.

Waka 75 A storm

a storm so violent
waka and coracles slam into each other
tohunga and filiddh swap notes
sing each other's airs
and before you know it the bloodlines
race in and out at crazy angles

Rangitoto surfaces lets out a breath
blood streams from pohutukawa
all at once
haka chanting fills the ocean
fish come up simultaneously raise their mouths
clouds make the shapes of ancient creatures
dinosaurs moa great eagles
sea hardens while land dissolves to water

night arrives with more blood
but groaning not singing

pigs squeal at the crater rim
pork boulders juggled at the mouth
of a hot clown

the Tarawera waka glides by
death death fear of death
mystery waka

again the wave slaps his face
try harder
slaps him again
portray me as I am

[Handwritten annotations: "Irish small boat - wickerwork" (pointing to coracles); "Priest (Maori)" (pointing to tohunga); "Poet - gaelic" (pointing to filiddh); "lava volcano" (pointing to Rangitoto); "tree (X-Mas)" (pointing to pohutukawa)]

Tangaroa slams his pint on the bar,
'Gissa nother,' he hisses – the bartender jumps,
slides a frothy wave the length of the bay –
the crowd of fur seals resume their conversations,
slapping each other on the backs.

A guy with a waka attitude walks in,
leans over looking at Tangaroa –
'I'll have what the wet guy's having
since he's gonna pay for it.'
The fur seals fly in all directions.

Tangaroa looks him up and down,
checks out his moko and his waka.
'You're one of Tane's kids, ain't ya.
That means we're kin!'
He pays for the drink.

Waka 77

thin strip
of land

In pre-colonial times the crews would walk
across the isthmus near Otahuhu to cross harbours,
carrying the waka.

If they were visible today
there would be motorcades, policemen
to control the crowds and traffic –
probably tv crews too,

perhaps a *Holmes* special. They'd probably
make it part of an Ironman event.
That's good, that's how it should be.
But they don't.

In olden days Mr Pene said at school
the waka would carry deceased across
from Mangere. But instead of burying them

at Maungakiekie they buried them at caves
in Onehunga, which was closer. That's why
Mangere is called Mangere which means lazy.

The dead ancestors must be there still.
Waiting for their trip to the great pa,
wanting the waka to return.

In the New Zealand Wars,
among the lives lost – civilians
and fighters – among the torched homes,
brutalities, manhunts, relatives
turned on each other,
amid the creeping through lines on bellies,
captured and wounded,
the horror of soldiers at the injustices,
the shared and alien customs of war,
amid the tired feet of horses and men
hauling artillery down the Great South Road,
amid the teeth of men – the military diet,
talk, bare lips and beards and moustaches,
amid the Maori men and women
who fought for themselves
let alone their culture, amid the torture
of death for all people who are left
to cope with the departure of the dead,
amid the context of Grey's second
governorship and his belligerent settler PM,
amid the context of a minor colony
draining Imperial coffers, Imperial forces,
amid the resistance of souls
to becoming the essence of souls,
the Empire took the waka.
They broke them where they confiscated them.
Burnt them. The iwi hid the old ones
we have today. Or built them again.
They had the psychological template.

Waka 79

Uncle Sam carved my mother a model waka –
he reached into history and pulled it out
from all the symbols available.

I have tried to draw a waka with words,
but it is becalmed by its own weight,
and the grunting of its maker.

stop
progress of

Uncle Sam's work is not for sale.

Peter Robinson created a painting
of many waka – white ones – among
the fleet there is a brown one, depicting
his Maori descent.

If I had an eight waka fleet
five would be Maori.

My Grandmother Sarah's mother,
of Kai Tahu and Kati Mamoe descent.
Her father was Scottish.
My Grandfather James's parents were Irish,
their forebears probably used coracles.

My Grandfather Massey's parents
who were of Ngati Kahu and Ngati Manu.
My Grandmother Matekino's parents,
of Ngati Hau and Ngati Whatua.

If I had a fleet of sixteen,
ten would be Maori.

If I had a fleet of thirty-two,
twenty would be Maori.

If I had a fleet of sixty-four,
forty would be Maori.

Then eighty. A hundred and sixty.
Three hundred and twenty.

To the beginning
of the Maori people.

I have parts of these genealogies written
linking parts of me with different waka.

Unfortunately, and it's a real regret,
I can go back only a little way
with my Irish and Scottish inheritance.

Waka 81 A cup of tea

At Harvest in Grey Lynn among
the alternative medicines and groceries

I saw they sell kumarahou leaves.   — shrub / tree
I wasn't thinking on my feet.

I'd bought sarsparilla and arnica
for my gout, but I hadn't thought

clearly – kumarahou man,
kumarahou is rongoa, Maori medicine,

remedy

good for the soul and cleansing
the poisons from your system.

The poison of mortgage stress.
Poison of material jealousy.

Poison of cycles of obsession.
These being poisons to do with the chest.

It could make me a new man,
give me the strength to row a waka.

91

Waka 82 *Te ao marama III*

i

Whatonga followed his grandfather Toi
to Aotearoa aboard Kurahaupo. He sailed

the Pacific to reach the man. He followed
the coasts (west and east) of the new land

to catch word of the man. Toi
must have been very proud,
very moved, to see his grandson.

ii

This second account is of a waka
designed for migration. Some claim

it was enchanted and wrecked.
A reef remains where the timber

may still be seen.
There are many different versions
and places for this waka.

Waka 83

I ask you, waka, ark, high altar
above the sea, your next destination?

Tangi, tangi throughout the land,
I am in demand to take souls to Hawaiiki
to satisfy the honour of spirits.

Take me to Hawaiiki.
Make an exception for one who breathes.

I will take you while you sleep.
You will see phosphorescent waves,
do not be frightened. Whale spouts
will hold the balls of your feet.
You will see the first Mount Hikurangi.
Swim in the Healing Spring of Tane
where the moon sleeps.
You will hear the elevated speech
of those who observe the destinies
driving the bodies of the people,
and all the stories buried there
like sacristies. People will float
like birds, fish will glitter, every cave
and waterfall a musical instrument –
a place too good to be true,
a place the navigators were searching for,
the home of their dreams,
only in their dreams.

And when I woke I was in my study typing.

[handwritten margin note:] funeral mourning song

Waka 84

I am the waka of memory,
unnamed, the template –

place me:

in Hawaiiki
in vehicles

in the mountains reefs cliffs
whare nui trees boulders

[handwritten: larger big/many]

in the words of the world Maori

I am the waka made a tree again

by a huge chrysalis of insects
by clearing the marks of humans

anger of these humans in particular

to be free in a forest
without the deadweight of this crew

oh I must feel sad for them
but it is hard being a waka alone

better to be a tree in a forest
a life marked by the chopping of tui

[handwritten: thread? bird?]

instead of adzes

[handwritten: similar to axe, cuts + shapes wood]

94

Waka 85

I am the star Kopua,
Venus to the colonials

and their explorers. I watched their tube eyes
watch me, one eye at a time.

. . .

We are cousins of Kopua,
Maahutonga, Southern Cross.

We have many points
and have been used throughout ages

belonging to humans
and creatures on other planets.

Light travels slowly
from great distances. So

our deliberation helped the navigators
travel quickly and safely to their homelands.

Sometimes we are obscured by clouds
and the navigators rely on other skills

such as translating the ripples
made when waves touch land

into a direction

Waka 86

I am Kupe. I have the credit for finding
this new land, the parts of which

I named with parts of me, including
my son – I have left my son here,

the gods were appeased.
My soul will never forget this.

I have been quoted many times,
e hoki a Kupe? Did Kupe return?

The saying is meant to politely
refuse a request. But I do

return to this land. Thoughts
I placed here keep returning

to my ears. I am sorry
for correcting the saying,

but I have been returning
for a very long time now.

I am the anonymous settler
fresh off the boat from Bristol,
arrived from a developed land
where the landscape
is landscaped, seating churches
and palaces, melodious clock towers,
aristocrats and Ascot, a land
                              where everything
has a place including the people.

Here we have tents and take food
from savages. The town is squatter
than Sydney. The *English* do not know
their stations any more.
My family will spend the next
century building this country
into a new England, and building
the mythology of England as home.

Waka 88

Do not mind the settler. I observe
the rules of this mythology (see how he did not

place a star or ocean or a waka
in his pageantry). I am Odysseus,

summoned to these pages by extraordinary
claims of the narrator. I run through all narratives.

Dr Jung put me there early in the century.
Look closely at the narration. Who

is holding the sails taut, commanding the paddles,
seeing that the carvings follow the patterns

of waka that follow the patterns of the sea?
I. Odysseus. I have put myself here

because this is a text. A very Western text.
The navigators sail with me now.

I sail as a member of the crew,
and can speak for them.

Waka 89

Yo I'm Maui. This facet is the Maui of the hauling.
The great fish is mine. I have first rights

and I am expressing anger ANGER ANGER
at being denied a significant portion of the text

of the Star Waka. The copyrights are mine.
Without me the waka would be a vaka for instance.

They wouldn't have a base, a matrix to tie
their culture to. You know I fished the land up

don't you? You know I placed it under the path
of Kopua, not far from Matariki, don't you?

How else would anyone find it?
What do you mean there'd be another star,

or birds? I tell you I put it there because those stars
are the best ones in the sky. I want credit.

And no more anthropologists.
I belong to cosmology. Dig, Odysseus?

Waka 90 Te ao marama IV

This is my third appearance. I am
Kurahaupo Waka. This time

I have taken the task
of representing the two hundred

waka remembered by the people,
shot to the cold regions here

by accounts turned to legends,
such is the elevated nature of oral literature.

I have been appointed by the narrator.
I am unelected, as is the narrator.

My appearance here is strange,
without the adornments of my mana,

the finery of inlaid carved and seasoned wood,
the ceremonial decorations taking me

into the sea. It's like journeying in a bathtub,
the margins of the sea of text

only released by the narrator's dreams.
And he doesn't write when he's asleep.

But my mana isn't in my physicality.
It's in the psyche of the culture that bred me.

Waka 91 A Feast

i

Stones are laid beneath the pyres
till they encompass the heat which
feeds through the layers of bird flesh
root vegetables smoking and steaming
underground – a hundred birds
a thousand vegetables oiling
the throats of the waka community

licking sucking chewing biting

ha-ha

a feast of the season

ii

scraps for the slaves
are heaped like atolls

rain makes goblets of their faces

Waka 92

I am an island
in the people's consciousness
storms foretell arrival of waka
carrying companies of strange birds
strangled by the breeze

each triangulation of sails
tells of trouble in the colonies
a fleet and there has been a great calamity
for I am an island of death

waka are hearses not vehicles for exploration
I gladly take them

they send the loved ones here

with some knowledge

of what it is to be a Maori

the others go to the other human place

called the collective unconscious

I am called Hawaiiki

Waka 93

My face is broken by the waves.
I am the sea, ocean, giver and taker,
primordial pre-culture pre-life.

To define me is to limit me,
one may as well define the planet.

Yet I am delicate, can feel a piece of wood
slip across my eye, can feel the calls
of men rowing as they dip into me

as if I was a well to scoop from.
Some of these I have taken
into the waters of my being.

So I am part human.

Waka 94

I am Tane Mahuta – and not offended
to be introduced at this late stage.

This is Tangaroa's story. I merely supply
the vessels. They are a small chink

in the arsenal of Tane. I command mountains,
influence the rain, the presence of my legions

directs Tangaroa's motions (you know,
from space you see clouds amass above

my forests, my children). I am a long-term
kind of god, not drawn into quick effect.

It is suitable that I am placed near the end
of the Star Waka, to emphasise my length.

I am Tangaroa, Lord of this domain
Star Waka travels. The sky
is my only mirror. I pluck people
for the ridge-pole tekoteko of my mighty whare.
I am kind.
I allow the carvings to talk to one another
about the lives they represent,
occasionally let them change
the stories. Tane may boast
about his size, but I
am the only one to rival the size
of our parents. He took them away
from one another – even though
they are big, an immensity each of them,
their love came immensely too.
It breaks them into bits and pieces
from the heavens – all of them –
to the tiniest piece of Papatuanuku.
I felt this as their closest child.
Star Waka, do not be fooled by Tane,
betraycr of my beloved parents,
come dive into the sea – here
I will send waves – don't deny me
you won't be spared because
my waves can turn land over to water
in a thrashing horrible instant.
Give up. I am Tangaroa
owner of the feasts of the sea
the harvester of deities
and you the crew of a little waka
shelter on a dead fish's back!

Waka 96

I am the star waka
guided by the left eyes
of the ancestors
in our black heaven.

Sometimes I carry stars
to Hawaiiki for release
into the night.

Sometimes I continue
the explorations
begun by our expeditions

into knowledge.
I have been sent back
to retrieve crops

and I have returned.
I have been sent
into the furthest corners

of the realms of the Pacific,
brought kumara
from Peru, carted stories

of crews gone into the dust
of the black heaven
inhabited by your father,

and under the cloak
of his protection,
and through the encouragement

of his wife, the mother of all beings,
I deny you, Tangaroa.
I will not sink beneath you today.

Waka 97

Pray for the crew
to row in unison
lift and dip exactly
hear the sound
of the chant

hoea hoea ra

pray for the crew
to know where to go
for their priests clear heads
sense to ration food
fill gourds

hoea hoea ra

pray for the lashings
and bailers and anchors
for the fish catch and big catch
to climb onto land
pray for remembering ritual

hoea hoea ra

bless this crew and their waka knowledge
bless this ship and its journeying
bless families about to part
bless the new land
bless the deities we bring

hoea hoea ra

Waka 98

waka images cut in and out
collages on the eyes
                below the eyebrows
popping up in legends
          coming out in urban myth
waka wallpaper
waka duvet covers
what dread hand shaped your fearful symmetry?
tiger of the sea carrying deities
to an empty land filled with fur seals
fat birds tall birds and mice
when will you stop tasting the wind?

when the wind relinquishes its salt taste
then like my ancient cousins I will turn to stone
and stay here forever

Waka 99

If waka could be resurrected
they wouldn't just come out
from museum doors smashing
glass cases revolving and sliding
doors on their exit

they wouldn't just come out
of mountains as if liquidified
from a frozen state
the resurrection wouldn't just
come about this way

the South Island turned to wood
waiting for the giant crew
of Maui and his brothers
bailers and anchors turned back
to what they were when they were strewn

about the country by Kupe
and his relations
the resurrection would happen
in the blood of the men and women
the boys and girls

who are blood relations
of the crews whose veins
touch the veins who touched the veins
of those who touched the veins
who touched the veins

who touched the veins
of the men and women from the time
of Kupe and before.
The resurrection will come
out of their blood.

Waka 100

Stroke past line 1642
into European time.
Stroke past 1769
and the introduction of the West

Stroke on the approach to 1835
and formal Northern Maori sovereignty.

Stroke into the New World and stop.

Crews alight, consign waka
to memory, family trees, remove
the prowed tauihu, drape
the feathered mana
around the whare-womb
of the next crew

who are to remember waka
into the beginning
of centuries years minutes hours seconds
long and short hands centred
on Greenwich

each person
of waka memory
to hold their thoughts,
each person of seagoing
and waterborn descent
whose hard waka
are taken away.

And years later,
we ask our ancestors to wake,
whose mokopuna are carving in eyes,
restoring chiselled features, mouths

coming out of wood, genitals,
feet planted
on shoulders winding into stars
on ceilings, our ancestors of a culture
that has held its breath
through the age of Dominion.
We've adzed waka out for them –
the memories, intricate knowledge,
fleet leaders, our reasons for being –
shoulders that carried so many waka –
summoning souls of myriads
of names above hundreds
of waka names.

And you waka, who have seen heaven,
the guts of the ocean, brought terror
and pleasure, who have exhausted
your crews of home thoughts
who have lifted songs above
the waves of the greatest and deepest ocean,

rise – rise into the air – rise to the breath –
rise above valleys into light and recognition –
rise where all who have risen
sing your names.

And you, Urizen, Jupiter, Io Matua Kore,
holder of the compasses –
wind compass, solar compass,
compass encompassing known
currents, breather of the first breath
in every breathing creature,
guide the waka between islands,
between years and eyes of the Pacific
out of mythologies to consciousness.

And you stars, the ancestors,
nuclear orbs, red giants, white dwarves,
burn brilliantly, burn on the waka down there,
burn on waka riding valleys,
burn on waka on mountain summits,
burn on waka in the night,
burn on waka past the end of the light.